THE MFR COACH'S GUIDE TO

HAVING YOUR OWN
MYOFASCIAL
RELEASE BUSINESS

HEATHER HAMMELL
www.themfrcoach.com

Heather Hammell
www.themfrcoach.com

Printed in the United States of America
First Printing 2020
First Edition 2020

10 9 8 7 6 5 4 3 2 1

HAVING YOUR OWN
MYOFASCIAL
RELEASE BUSINESS

Table of Contents

Thank You...

When I set out to write this book, I knew that I wanted to help MFR therapists have an easier transition into a full-time MFR business. I wasn't sure I had enough to say or the right words, but I decided to put everything I knew down on paper. In the end, it was just the right amount of information.

Anyone should be able to pick up this book and take action. I don't know if I would have had the courage to write this if it wasn't for the training and mentorship I have received from John Barnes over the last ten years.

MFR has changed my life by allowing me to believe in myself and have my own back. Thank you, John, for giving me the time, and for teaching me to believe it's **all** possible. For anyone reading this book, it's **all** possible for you too.

Contact Information

Email:

Heather@themfrcoach.com

Website:

www.themfrcoach.com

Warmly, Heather Hammell

A Message from The Author

My business coach recently said, "Business is just math and drama. How many offers are you making to clients and how many no's are you getting?"

There is an equation to figure out the number of Yeses (paying clients) you are getting:

(# of offers) - (# of No's) = (The # of paying clients/Yeses).

It's that simple. The drama you have in your head prevents you from talking about what you do and making offers to help people. Sometimes it's because you don't feel like you know how to talk about it in a way that people fully understand. Sometimes it's because you are just too worried about what other people will think of you.

When I first went into business for myself, I didn't realize all the things that make a business successful. I also didn't realize how long it would take to figure it out along the way. It wasn't until I was many years into running my business that I realized other people out in the world know more than me about this. Not only that, but there are people that can tell me what to do—step by step—and what to avoid so that I can just do my work, get paid, grow, and help people.

The seminar that changed my life...

I had a small but successful massage practice going when I went to my first MFR seminar.

The seminar that changed my life.

I did not head into that seminar knowing the impact it would have. I went with two other massage therapists, and you know what?

Both of them are still doing massage therapy, charging $60 an hour and doing business as usual. Meanwhile, I have gone on to take every seminar, most of them at least three times, and now I charge three times the amount they do—women who learned the same thing I did at the same time.

The only difference is that massage was not enough for me. I believed I could help more people and make more money and live a different life than I had first thought.

Believe in yourself and go for it; nothing is sweeter than doing the thing you want to do.

I became an expert over time, simply because I chose to, took the steps, and followed through.

If you are reading this, you have also likely decided—or are in the process of deciding—to fully invest in yourself and your clients and become an MFR therapist exclusively.

There are no guarantees in life and no one can promise how things will turn out, but I know that when I've really gone all in, there wasn't a way for me to fail—because I refused to.

I might not have done things perfectly, but I always learned on the journey.

I'm sharing all my business knowledge with you so you don't make the same mistakes and can get there faster, with less doubt, confusion, and worry.

You may worry that you will lose all your regular massage clients—and yes, you might, but you will refill your practice with the clients that you want. It can happen quicker than you think, especially when you know all the tips and tricks to make that happen.

This book is a guide to help you go from running your massage business to running a successful MFR practice. You can be the MFR therapist that sees their ideal clients, understands their needs, offers them the outcomes they want, and earns money that not only pays the bills but lets you thrive. I'll share with you exactly how I did it so that you can take that knowledge and go.

You don't have to wait for a different circumstance or the perfect timing. You can get to work now, building the business you desire, no matter where you live or the acronym that follows your name.

This book will provide insight into just how easy it is to transition your business into a full-time MFR practice, even if you live in a tiny town, even if you don't know everything, and even if you don't already have a full practice. I say this to you with love: Your mind is going to tell you that you can't do it, and even your friends and family might say the same thing.

The only thing keeping you from doing it is your thoughts about it. I am here to help walk you through the process. I hope you will be able to gain the confidence and knowledge you need to get going, so you can be out in the world helping as many clients as possible.

If this book leaves you wanting more, I'm here to help you with that too. I coach MFR therapists and guide them on how to start and run businesses with less drama, less confusion, and more accountability to do what they want and to get the clients they want.

So you want to be an MFR Therapist

You've completed your first MFR seminar, or maybe you've completed quite a few, and you now know that your regular massage business just isn't going to cut it for you anymore.

You've realized that your clients will benefit more from MFR than massage, and you are starting to think about how to make the switch. You aren't sure how to explain what MFR is and you aren't confident enough in your skills to pull this off.

You've considered getting on the JFB directory, but you think you should wait until you are advanced or an expert before you commit to that.

During MFR 1, John often says, "You know enough to be better than any other therapist out there right now. Go out into the world and do it. Don't wait."

He's always right.

We put undue pressure on ourselves to be perfect at what we are doing before we are willing to take a risk.

I challenge you to challenge this belief of perfection.

Can you help someone with your MFR skills today?

You can.

But only if you offer it and then do MFR.

NO EXCUSES...

When I found MFR ten years ago, I was running a small massage business and raising little kids. My husband was trying to recover from a back injury from which he had suffered for nearly five years.

I knew right away, at my first seminar (fascial pelvis in Sedona), that MFR could help my husband. I decided, right then and there, that this was for me!

That feeling is what we want to help capture in all of your clients so that they want MFR for themselves.

I started talking about MFR all the time, and I still do. I took as many seminars as I could, which ended up being a lot. I'm not sure how I made it work back then.

I had a 5-year-old, a 3-year-old, and a 1-year-old, and my husband had to lay on the ground to do his work.

I'm telling you this because we all have excuses about why we can't get to seminars, can't afford it, don't have time, or whatever the reasons are.

If you decide this is for you, decide not to have an excuse. Decide it is what you are doing.

Trust me, you will make it work. Whatever decision you make, you   are   right.

Story

What is it about MFR that speaks to you?

_____

_____

_____

_____

_____

_____

_____

_____

_____

_____

_____

_____

_____

_____

_____

Why do you want to be an MFR therapist?

Why is this important to you?

What is your mission?

How has MFR helped you, a loved one, or a client?

Using your story...

Once you are clear on these answers, the way you talk to clients and a wider audience about what you do and why you do it will become easier and more repeatable.

So write down your answers, see how they make you feel, edit, and rewrite until you feel the passion and excitement that you usually feel at a seminar. Use words that you can easily say without getting confused or causing confusion to someone who has never been to a seminar before.

Then, start practicing. Every time you meet someone new and they ask what you do, say you're an MFR therapist and tell them your story.

Even if you are awkward at first, it's okay. We all are when we are beginners.

The more practice you get, the easier it will become to talk about what you do.

Watch the reactions of the people you talk to.

Do they glaze over or do they engage and ask you questions?

Tweak your story as you go to avoid the glazed-over look.

Your Ideal Client (1)

Who is your ideal client? How do you even figure this out? We are going to go through a series of questions here. Answer them to the best of your ability. I'd suggest writing these answers down so you can refer back to them later.

1. WHO DO YOU PICTURE YOURSELF WORKING WITH?

_____

_____

_____

_____

_____

_____

_____

_____

_____

_____

_____

_____

_____

_____

2..WHAT IS THEIR AGE?

3..WHAT PROBLEMS DO THEY HAVE?

4..DO THEY HAVE MONEY TO PAY FOR TREATMENT?

Your Ideal Client (2)

Continue answering questions about your ideal client . Think of all of the possible information to know about them.

5..DO THEY HAVE TIME FOR TREATMENT?

_____

_____

_____

_____

_____

_____

_____

_____

_____

_____

_____

_____

_____

_____

6..WHAT ELSE DO YOU KNOW ABOUT THEM?

Your ideal client might change after you go through this exercise, and that is okay.

Do not skip this step if you believe your ideal client is easy because **everybody** needs MFR.

Yes, everyone can benefit from MFR, but they are not all the correct fit for you.

By narrowing your ideal client down, you can speak directly to them and in return, you get to work with the people you enjoy the most.

Does this mean you turn away random people that don't fall into your ideal? No, but if your business is full of your ideal people, you could refer the people that don't fit to other therapists.

The world is large and you can pick whoever you want.

Just pick something and stick to it. This will help target your marketing efforts, which will minimize the amount of money you spend to attract new clients.

Seeking out your ideal clients will also help to avoid burnout.

When you go to work every day, excited about who you are going to be seeing, it has a different feel to it than going to work to see people who you don't want to be seeing or working with.

"YOUR IDEAL CLIENT IS NOT EVERYONE"

Why your ideal client is ideal...

It is important to understand and love your reasons for choosing your ideal client.

I was interviewing an MFR therapist and I asked about plans for getting his business started.

He told me that he had just spent roughly six hundred dollars on a software system so he could process insurance claims for motor vehicle accident patients.

We chatted about insurance and what it takes to file for reimbursement and if an MVA client is really his preferred client. During this chat, I asked him many questions.

"Do you want to be treating people that are coming to you because someone else is paying for it?

Do you think they will be the most committed to getting better? Do you want to treat people who will quit once insurance isn't paying for treatment?

Do you want to spend your free time doing extra paperwork that you do not get paid to do?"

Ease vs Effort

Later, I asked who the ideal person he wanted to work with was, and he answered without skipping a beat.

"I want to treat people that are in the mental health field. So psychiatrists, psychologists, social workers, and counselors.

Those people that really need to keep their bodies going because they are busy and working hard and have money to spend."

Trust me, the energy behind this answer compared to the insurance response was pure genius. There is nothing that will stop this therapist from reaching his goals if he follows through on the vision of his ideal client.

Once he could picture who he wanted to work with, he could directly market to those people instead of wasting time hoping to get reimbursed by insurance companies—a job that would have taken a lot of time and effort.

I asked him if he could charge these people what he would have been reimbursed with insurance and he thought he could. All of a sudden, this cleared up a lot of chaos and confusion he had been feeling about where to begin his business and to whom he should market   his   services.

Work Smarter, Not Harder

In the next chapters, we will talk about rates and knowing how to set them to earn income, but here is what else I told this therapist:

"You can see the number of clients you want and get paid what you want versus getting paid less and working harder on patients you aren't excited to see. If you are making plenty of money to pay your bills and yourself, then you can choose to offer discounts or free sessions to anyone else you feel like helping, because you will have the freedom to do so and it will come from something really good.

"It won't be coming from the desperation to get the client through your door. Your ideal client won't need any convincing."

Your Messaging

I HELP (YOUR IDEAL CLIENT) TO ACHIEVE (THESE RESULTS).

Your ability to communicate about MFR and what it can provide your patients is key to not only your success but—most importantly—the success of your clients.

Your client does not care about what MFR is, but they care about the results.

So being crystal clear on what those results will be is the first step. "I help (Your Ideal Client) to achieve (these results)."

This is going to vary, but I will provide you with a few examples:

I help busy psychiatrists maintain their heavy schedules by eliminating migraines and body pain so they can continue to show up for their patients.

I help women of ages forty through sixty stay active by reducing back and neck pain so they can keep weight off, keep up with their children and grandchildren, and feel good throughout their day.

I help patients with chronic pain reduce their need for pain medication by eliminating the source of their pain through the use of MFR. Reduced pain medication helps to be more present in their lives, allows for regular bowel movements, and helps them feel good again.

Your Messaging

HOW DO YOU HELP YOUR CLIENT?

Decide how you help them; what you use MFR to help them get.

Not what you do to help them, but what the outcome is. This might feel weird at first, but just keep practicing.

The more you say it, the easier and more natural it will feel.

This will help you when selling your plan of care to your clients as well. You will sell them on the outcome, not the method to get them there.

When you buy plane tickets, you aren't buying the plane ride, you're buying the destination.

You never hear Delta advertise to come and sit in their cramped cabin with germy people, no cabin service, and a bumpy ride.

All you are thinking about when making that purchase is laying on the beach at your destination or hugging the loved ones you meet when you land.

Keep that in mind when you are talking to clients. We are not selling that plane ride, we are selling the results after they land.

They are going to feel better, move better, enjoy their lives more, participate in the activities that they love, and feel good while doing it.

Your Messaging

ARE YOU SPEAKING THEIR LANGUAGE?

Language is also important.

I always felt so good and smart about formally talking about fascia, with big words like PiezoElectric and Collagenous barrier... but do you know what clients hear?

They hear Charlie Brown's teacher talking and they don't (for the most part) give a shit.

Explain to them what you do and why you do it in terms a third-grader could understand.

Example:

"I will be holding everything for five minutes or longer because research proves that fascia (the organ we are intending to make changes with) can only be influenced by time and pressure.

"Five minutes is a while, so it might seem like we are not doing very much, but a lot is happening underneath my hands, deep in your body.

"Your body is releasing anti-inflammatory properties right to the areas that need it most, which will reduce pain and increase your body's ability to heal."

Some clients will want to ask a lot of questions about what exactly you are doing.

In those cases, use all of your big, fancy words and nerd out. When you are speaking to potential clients, just keep it basic. "I deliver these results..."

Focus on their needs and how you can get the results they are looking for. This provides a good amount of clarity and confidence. Your client will be interested in getting that outcome for   themselves.

The Drama You Have About Your Skill Level

It does not take an expert-level MFR therapist to be an expert at running an MFR business.

It takes someone willing to understand their client, create a clear message, offer a result your ideal client is seeking and willing to pay for, and someone who can make decisions and take massive action to get results.

You could wait to practice MFR and take every single seminar.

You could take one seminar and call yourself an MFR therapist.

You could take a few seminars and practice as you go, learning and growing your skillset.

Being an MFR therapist requires a very specialized skill set.

I encourage you to learn it well, follow the principles, and make it work for your practice.

Take as many seminars as you can, and keep taking them. **And** get a lot of treatment for yourself.

The best therapists are the ones that respect their own bodies by treating them with the best therapy there is—and that is MFR. Get   a   T4T.

Get Treated!

Go to study groups or create a study group. Don't settle for only the treatment at seminars.

It's really fun, but it isn't real treatment.

If this is you, stop doing that and book some appointments.

Do it even if you have to travel for it. If you aren't willing to pay and travel for MFR therapy, why would any of your clients be willing to pay and/or travel to you for it?

I have so much respect for therapists that don't know it all. They continue to learn, get treated, and work each day with a little bit of wonder and a lot of awe in the results they are creating for their clients.

It's very rewarding to help someone end their pain and enjoy their life again.

I can't wait for you to experience it, and if you already have, I hope you never take for granted how fun it is.

This chapter is to tell you that you just need to start. Just decide that you are going to start doing MFR and then do it, without worry or judgment.

Even if you have been a very successful massage therapist for the last twenty years, you can completely switch to MFR and love your new business. When this is clearly what you want to do, it will be easier to do it.

The hardest part will be making the decision and navigating the mind drama you will create—the little voice that says it's scary or that you can't do it because people will still want a massage.

Pricing Mistakes—Understanding Personal and Business Finances

RATES AND KNOWING HOW TO SET THEM TO EARN INCOME

You can see the number of clients you want and get paid the amount you want.

Many therapists I have interviewed get paid less and work harder on patients they aren't excited to see because they feel like they have to keep their rates low or risk losing clients.

This is a belief.

You can also choose to believe that you can get paid what you want and still have **all** the clients you need.

This is where having a coach really helps you get your mind/money thoughts headed in a healthier direction. It's easy to get into a thought loop about money.

MAKE MONEY FIRST

Once you are making plenty of money to pay your bills and yourself, you can then choose to offer discounts or free sessions, because you will have the freedom to do so. It will come from something really good, instead of desperation to get the client through the door. Your ideal client won't need any convincing.

Understand Your Finances

I once interviewed an MFR therapist who told me she set her prices based on the lowest rate a massage therapist in her small town charged because she thought massage was a luxury.

My eyeballs popped out of my face.

This, my friends, is **not** how we set our rates. This doesn't make sense on any business level.

Before we go any further into money, I recommend investing in a program like Profit U. Use this link to sign up and take this very helpful class: https://www.profitucourse.com/profit-u/842w1

With this online program, you get an exact way to organize both your business and personal finances. It is easy, step by step, and super detailed on spreadsheets you can keep and edit. It's fascinating what you can do when you know where you are and where you want to go.

Know where you are financially in business and your personal life. The 'head in the sand' approach has no place in real business. Guessing or assuming is also not okay.

You need to know exactly what is happening so you can make strategic decisions and own a business instead of owning a job. Rates are going to vary but having a simple formula is a good place to start.

First things first: write down all your expenses. Use the columns on the next page. Collect information on your personal expenses (family/household bills, etc.) in one column and then do a column for your business expenses.

How many hours are you available to treat your clients per day? Per week? How many hours do you want to be treating clients?

How many hours do you need per week to do office tasks?

Do you want to hire office staff, such as a front desk person?

Take the time to write all of the answers out. Go over them and weed out things you don't need to be paying for, like unwanted subscriptions.

Account for your goals with training for the year to make sure you can cover those expenses as well.

Writing it all down

DO NOT SKIP THIS STEP

LEFT SIDE PERSONAL EXPENSESRIGHT SIDE BUSINESS EXPENSES

mortage/rent

_____

lease/mortgage

_____

car payment

_____

internet

_____

food

_____

insurance

_____

clothing

_____

laundry

_____

insurance:

_____

scheduling software

_____

Writing it all down

DO NOT SKIPTHISSTEP

LEFT SIDE PERSONAL EXPENSESRIGHT SIDE BUSINESS EXPENSES

Writing it all down

DO NOT SKIPTHISSTEP

LEFT SIDE PERSONAL EXPENSESRIGHT SIDE BUSINESS EXPENSES

Writing it all down

DO NOT SKIPTHISSTEP

LEFT SIDE PERSONAL EXPENSESRIGHT SIDE BUSINESS EXPENSES

Figuring it out...

DO NOT SKIP

1. . HOW MANY HOURS ARE YOU AVAILABLE FOR
TREATMENT?

2. . HOW MANY CLIENTS PER DAY?

3. . PER WEEK?

4. . HOW MANY HOURS DO YOU WANT TO BE TREATING CLIENTS?

5. . HOW MANY HOURS DO YOU NEED PER WEEK TO DO OFFICE TASKS?

_____

_____

_____

_____

_____

_____

_____

_____

_____

_____

_____

_____

_____

_____

_____

_____

_____

6. . DO YOU WANT TO HIRE OFFICE STAFF LIKE A FRONT DESK PERSON?

_____

_____

_____

_____

_____

_____

_____

_____

_____

_____

_____

_____

_____

_____

_____

_____

_____

_____

Pain Points

THOUGHT DOWNLOAD

Write down all of the things you do not like doing in your business or that you think will make you uncomfortable once you have a business.

Here are a few I have gathered through my interview with MFR Therapists:

Exchanging money with clients—Scheduling/reminding clients of appointments—No-shows—Laundry—Cleaning—Burnout—Undercharging

When you know your pain points, you can set yourself up to afford to have help with them and/or set things up with automated systems.

_____

_____

_____

_____

_____

_____

_____

_____

_____

_____

_____

_____

_____

_____

The Reluctant Business Owner

NOTICE WHERE YOU HAVE ISSUES AND TAKE STEPS TO RESOLVE YOUR ISSUES AROUND BUSINESS.

WE LIKE TO HELP PEOPLE, RIGHT? THAT'S WHY WE DO WHAT WE DO. MANY THERAPISTS TELL ME THEY ARE SO HORRIFIED BY THE THOUGHT OF EXCHANGING MONEY AT THE END OF A SESSION THAT THEY UNDERPRICE THEIR SERVICES JUST SO THEY CAN SLEEP AT NIGHT.

Work on your issues around money or you will never feel good when it is time to get paid at the end of a session.

This fearful mindset will affect your business at a very deep level. It's toxic thinking.

There are some decisions here that can be made ahead of time and practiced over and over again to make the money exchange feel better.

I interviewed another MFR therapist who told me that she has gotten so good at selling, it's her favorite part of the job. Now she's selling so much, she has to be careful so she can have enough time to treat all the clients she is bringing on.

She has a fun mindset that is seriously dedicated to helping her clients see the results and want it every time. And if they don't, then they probably weren't her ideal client, so that's a good result too. Her process weeds out clients that aren't dedicated and aren't ready for the healing she can provide.

She educates, makes offers to help, and over-delivers every time. She has so much energy for her clients because she is excited about all of the processes she has set up.

I used to feel uncomfortable taking money from clients too, but I got some help with that and decided I love money and figuring out how to create more money all the time. I spend a lot of money on continuing education, travel, creating a beautiful treatment space, and creating a ton of value for the outcome I provide my clients.

GET HELP GETTING OVER YOUR FEARS ABOUT YOUR BUSINESS.

Standing Out In The Crowd

"YOU DIDN'T COME THIS FAR TO ONLY COME THIS FAR"

-JOHN F. BARNES

If you are an MFR therapist, you are not giving a massage.

I think there are over three hundred massage therapists in the town in which I practice, yet I am the only one doing MFR. If I charged for massage and advertised to massage clients, how am I any different?

MFR is completely different, and someone looking for a massage or relaxation is not my ideal client.

Is your ideal client the one that is price shopping or the one who wants to get better faster?

I'd pick the one who wants to get better over the price shopper any day.

I want dedicated clients who want what I'm selling. Everyone else can go get a massage or find someone cheaper who isn't offering what I am.

I didn't come this far to only come this far, and neither did you. You want to have success and you want to pay your bills and you want to go on vacation, right?

So, stop selling yourself short by undercharging to feel better about charging money in the first place.

It won't work, and you will end up being exhausted and burnt out because you will have to work harder.

"Who are you attracting into your business? Are you attracting them based on your own fears? Or based on decisions you've made to be able to have the business you want?"

The price you charge for Myofascial Release has nothing to do with your value.

If you charge $60 per session, only want to see four clients per day, and only want to work three days per week, that would be a maximum income of $720 per week.

If you charge $120 per session, see four clients per day, and work three days per week, it would be $1440.

Before taxes, you'd bring in $69,120.

You could get the same results at the $60 rate if you see twice as many clients per week. So, instead of four clients per day, you could do eight.

What do you think the long-term result of that would be?

Could you still see your kids' soccer game or your grandkids' musical if you work that much?

I say honor your body and your mind by deciding ahead of time how much and how often you are willing to treat clients. Then, set your price based on how much you need and want to earn.

Do not base this on your value.

Your value as a person is infinite and has nothing to do with the price you put on the service you offer.

Let that sink in. See how you feel when you realize your prices have nothing to do with you as a person and everything to do with how you pay expenses and earn a salary and still enjoy a life outside of work.

You might just make a different decision by thinking that way.

If you are still feeling resistant about charging what you need to reach your goals, then reach out. This is something that you could easily be coached on.

Three types of people...

There are different types of clients out there:

Cheaple (cheap people):

People who are price-shoppers, looking for the cheapest price for the service. They only care about cost, not the outcome.

Feeple (Fee for service people):

People who will pay a fee for the service but don't understand they are paying for an outcome.

Premple (Premium People):

People who will pay top dollar for the best service and best outcome possible.

Your clients are premium people who are willing to pay well, and you should be charging a premium rate.

It costs a significant amount of money to continue your education with classes like John F. Barnes' MFR seminars.

This is in addition to whatever schooling and certification you had before learning MFR.

As I said before, charge what your service is worth (it has nothing to do with your personal value—never has and never will) and over-deliver with results and value.

I always give my clients a self-treatment ball and access to a Facebook group full of self-treatment videos, just for being a client of mine. This is added value to the price of the sessions they purchased.

I also always start and end sessions on time. My clients know I will be there, ready to go when they come, and will get them out of treatment and on to their next destination as promised.

Time is valuable, both yours and the clients'.

Now, you might read this and get stuck thinking you still want to help everyone— that your prices should not hinder someone who can't   afford   it   from   getting   your   help.

What is your version of integrity in pricing?

Think about this:

If you charge what you want, make a salary that affords you to live a nice life, and aren't burned out at the end of the day, don't you think you could offer a way to treat people who can't afford it? You can do whatever you want!

You can offer free sessions! you can offer discounts or scholarships!

You are in control.

So, charging an amount that covers your expenses and makes you money does not make you a bad person.

Again, there is a lot of work you can do about your thoughts on this subject to help you get a clean and clear vision of what maintains integrity with your prices.

Do the work and get the help you need to get over the pricing drama. It's worth it, trust me. It's the difference between worrying about pricing at the end of your sessions every single day and never even thinking about it. Think of how much time you'd have and how awesome you'd feel if you didn't have mind drama around pricing.

Ask yourself what your version of keeping the integrity with your pricing looks like. Does it cover your bills? Are you helping people? Are you able to pay yourself?

If you can answer yes to these questions, you are pricing with integrity. If your answer to either of these questions is no, then you need to figure out what is happening.

SYSTEMS AND AUTOMATIONS

There are a lot of systems on the internet that you can use to make your business run more efficiently.

I have found that online services for tracking expenses, online appointment booking, credit card processing, and tracking client sessions to be the most helpful.

I have also invested in a laundry service. They pick up my dirty sheets and drop off clean and pressed sheets every week. It's not as expensive as you might imagine.

The amount of time you can save yourself by having someone else do the laundry is incredible. It might sound like a luxury, but it's something I am willing to pay for.

When I go home at the end of the day, I want to be home, not doing laundry. I already do plenty of laundry for my family. It felt like a total splurge when I started, but now I can't imagine not having it.

SYSTEMS YOU NEED TO HAVE

Online Scheduling is a necessity, even if you don't allow your clients to schedule themselves. If you don't want to do too much research into which system is best, I'll recommend going with the Massage Book. You get a webpage, clients can be scheduled online, and you can take and track payments, packages, sessions, and SOAP notes all in one spot. The cost is low, and they are constantly updating their platform and improving it.

Make it easy on you and your clients!

Clients get text and email reminders too, so they are much less likely to miss an appointment.

There is also an app so that your clients can make appointments themselves.

I love that clients can schedule themselves. You can always keep control and you can

give your link out to whomever you want.

You can keep control over the schedule that you like.

There are a lot of choices out there for scheduling.

Acuity, Simple Practice, Square, and Massage Book are some top selections.

Most of the time, you can get a free trial and check out all of the amenities to make sure it's a good fit for you and your practice.

The best choice is something easy for you and your clients to navigate, which also has features you want for tracking purposes and organization.

Accounting software is another necessity.

You need something that can capture your expenses from your business credit cards, business checking, and business savings accounts. Something that you can run reports from and can easily update.

I recommend using something like Freshbooks. It's very easy to operate and connects easily to your accounts. You can also use free software like MINT.com.

The important thing is to track all of your expenses and your income. By the end of the year, it can be very difficult to remember what was going on in January or April.

So track it all and check in weekly or bi-weekly to make sure things are accurate and syncing properly.

Make It Easy To Get Paid

KEEP GOOD RECORDS

Credit Card Processing:

Get a credit card processor. I recommend Square or Stripe accounts. It's good to have both, so if one system isn't working, you have a backup.

I believe both of these can connect to Massage Book and many other software systems. When you are charging a premium or offering packages, premium people like to charge and earn points with their credit cards, so let them.

The fees for taking credit cards are small, but you can also add them back into the price if you want to (if it is legal in your state).

Some people will always pay in cash or with a check. Let them. Make it easy to get paid.

YOUR WEBSITE

Create a simple website, designed specifically to target your ideal client, with ways for them to easily contact you.

The following screen grabs are from my latest MFR website. I took a class on how to make this work correctly. It cost a lot of money to get advice from a web design expert, but I'm going to just tell you everything I learned.

Just copy what I did.

Simplify your message.

The first page should explain exactly what you do in a simple sentence. This is the first thing your clients will see. Make the font large.

Have your logo in one corner (click to call would be a great add-on).

You want your sentence about what you do to be "above the fold" so it's basically a headline for your client's eyes to key in on. They should immediately understand exactly who you work with and what you do.

YOUR WEBSITE

The second thing you want your clients to see is a brief video of you explaining what you do.

Here is a screengrab of what that looks like. It isn't the most flattering thumbnail, but that's okay.

Clients are looking for people like them, so here I am, being super relatable. I don't think I was even wearing makeup in this video because I was just being sincere and unscripted.

After posting this video, I regularly got customers who mentioned it when they called to book appointments.

That's all you want—something that people can relate to and that gets them to call you.

Practice making your video and then go for it. Just get one made. You can always go back later and make a "better" one. Just be yourself and explain your story; why MFR means so much to you and what is possible for your clients. They really want to know this information and a video is a great way to explain things.

YOUR WEBSITE

At the bottom of the video, I have three buttons to help people decide to call me, learn more about the cost and availability, and book a discovery session (consultation).

These buttons are linked, to trigger an email response. They alert me to the potential clients' interest, captures their contact information, and adds them to my email lists, depending on what they are interested in.

The phone call button lets them know I will call them within twenty-four hours on a weekday or the next business day if they are inquiring on the weekend.

You could also just make that button instantly dial your office. Make it work for you. If you don't offer free discovery visits, then don't add that button. I repeat these buttons on every page. This encourages action to be taken by the person viewing the pages.

Here is another screen grab with lots of buttons and a small section on who we help and what we do. This is a shot of the "Our Programs" page.

YOUR WEBSITE/ BLOG PAGE

Notice that I have kept my website pretty simple. There are only five pages: Home,

About, Our Programs, Blog, and Contact.

Keeping it clean and simple keeps clients moving and making decisions to call, ask for more information, or schedule.

You can also leave a link for clients to schedule right from your website if you want to.

This screengrab is from my Blog page.

YOUR WEBSITE/ ABOUT PAGE

I have one page dedicated to my story. So, not only do I talk about it in the video, I wrote about it too.

This is another example of creating a way to connect with clients. If they can see that I understand them and know what their problems are, they are more likely to schedule with me. Take some time again and really work on your story. Be a great storyteller!

About Heather Hammell

My Story

In 2010 my husband, Dr. Abe Hammell, came home from a Naval deployment, injured, with a herniated disc in his lumbar spine. After a failed surgeries and then another surgery to replace a lumbar discs in his back, he was still living with chronic pain and taking a lot of medication just to survive his life. I completed Massage Therpy School and worked constantly to try to help decrease his pain with temporary results. He didn't get any better with traditional Physical Therapy either. We were so frustrated. In 2011, I found myself at a John Barnes Myofascial Release seminar. That seminar changed everything for both me and for my husband. After completing the seminar I went home and began treating Abe. He responded to the treatment immediately. We wanted to fast track his results, so we sent him to Sedona, AZ where he got 3 hours of Myofascial Release everyday for 2 weeks. Having gone to Sedona using a cane and the use of a wheel chair, he's never used assistive devices again.

Equipment

Massage Table	*Massage Table*	*Kneeling Chair*
I purchased an OakWorks Proluxe electric table for a very reasonable price about twelve years ago (before I was doing MFR).	If you want a portable table, the best options are something light, easy to set up, and very sturdy.	I like the kneeling chair when I am treating clients, but there are so many choices out there. Pick a chair that is comfy for you. Almost everything you want you can check out on Amazon.
The ability to move the table up or down at the touch of a button is genius.	You want it to be able to take your weight and the weight of your client if necessary.	
I can see various body types and always have the height exactly where I need it.	Most really good tables will set you back $500-800.	
It has also come in handy	I personally like the Strong Lite brand. My husband has	

HAVING YOUR OWN MYOFASCIAL RELEASE BUSINESS

for people in wheelchairs   had a table he used in

to be able to transfer with   medical school in 1997 and

ease. These sell for around   I still use it to see clients

$1500 currently.   when I travel.

POLICIES AND PROCEDURES

Policies and Procedures:

An important part of the client/therapist relationship is a clear understanding of your policies and procedures. A good place to start is your cancelation policy. Having a strict and transparent policy will prevent unwanted and unnecessary gaps in your schedule and will keep your clients from making careless no-shows or late cancelations for their sessions.

I have always had a strict no-refund policy on any package of sessions purchased and a use-by date. I only offer package discounts for those clients who bought six or more with the intention of booking and using them close together for quicker healing. It was not intended to be a discounted leisure use rate. Whatever policies you make up, just make sure they are signed off on by your clients and that they are understood.

Then when something happens, and it will, you can lose less money by having that in place from the beginning. You won't have to spend a lot of mental energy worrying about charging a late fee or imposing a penalty. Also, clients are less likely to no-show or run late when they know you are going to hold them accountable. No one wants to lose any money, so they will make it a priority even more with that incentive.

Forms and Paperwork

Forms and Paperwork: With online scheduling platforms like Massagebook, you can easily set up an online form for your Health History and intake. Have the client fill it out before they come in for treatment and save a ton of time on paperwork. The document is then stored in your account. Take SOAP notes; again, something like Massagebook will hold all of these documents for you, available at a touch of a button should something come up.

Insurance

Insurance: I have had both ABMP and AMTA and I like them both. They both offer various discounts. I have found that ABMP has more discounts that I actually use and they offer a discount with Massagebook as well, which is fantastic. I also carry another policy to protect my LLC.

Ask your insurance provider what they recommend. You don't need anything expensive but I do recommend carrying insurance to make sure you are protected. In many cases, you can carry unemployment insurance too, and then if something like COVID-19 happens again in the future, you won't have to depend on government-funded programs to provide self-employment unemployment. You will be able to get benefits right away.

In many states, it's required to carry this if you have employees or independent contractors working for you.

CHECK WITH YOUR LICENSING BOARD....

I want to remind you that you need to know and understand the rules for your individual licensure. If you are a PT, your rules and insurance needs will be different. Just make sure you investigate and understand the rules ahead of time.

Employees and/or Independent Contractors

"RELATIONSHIPS END AND FEELINGS GET HURT. HAVE A CONTRACT..."

If you decide you are going to have people work for you or with you, please-please-*please* make sure you have a contract that lays out the terms and expectations.

It might seem like you are both reasonable people and nothing could ever go wrong but trust me, things can go wrong even with the nicest and coolest people you could ever hope to hire.

It is not very expensive to have a lawyer draw up a contract for you (they can make one that can be edited, so you can use it over and over again for your new hires/new contractors as you grow).

I suggest getting a contract with your front desk person or virtual assistant too. Lay out all of your expectations from the beginning.

It is much harder to go back and change your mind once someone has started, so having this ahead of time is strongly recommended.

Questions you need to know the answers to:

1. Do you ever feel like if you just knew exactly how to explain what you do in simple terms, your ideal clients would understand more easily and want MFR all the time?

2. Do you question what you should charge your clients or feel bad about charging a price that allows you to pay your bills and earn a profit?

3. Do you have questions about getting your massage clients to become MFR clients?

4. Do you have fears around making a complete switch and doing only MFR, but know that it is what you want to do?

5. Do you know what you need on your website to attract your ideal clients?

6. Do you have systems in place to automate your schedule, billing, and appointment reminders?

7. Do you have policies for your practice for no-shows, late arrivals, or packages?

8. Are you charging enough to draw a salary with which you can live a great life and cover your expenses?

9. Are you getting regular treatment in addition to going to seminars?

10. Do you have an idea and a plan for when to take seminars?

11. Do you have specific goals for taking seminars?

One of the many benefits to hiring a coach who has been there and done that—as far as starting an MFR business goes—is that you can get going and set up faster and with a solid foundation with answers to these questions.

You don't have to do the trial and error of learning as you go because you have someone helping you and guiding you along the way.

You make all the decisions, but you understand why you make them and can come up with a strategy, get personalized support, and grow the practice of your dreams.

Ask anyone who has hired a coach, years into owning a business, and they will tell you that their businesses exploded afterward. The work you do on yourself and your mindset is the key to growing your business and busting out of the boxes we put ourselves in.

I hope your takeaway from reading this book and completing the exercises is that you can see how to operate and manage your business with ease and confidence. You are capable of running an empire, of earning enough money to live a fun life of generosity and ease.

I help MFR therapists become the business owners they didn't know they could be by helping them develop their messaging, identify their perfect client, and learn how to speak to clients.

If you are curious about what's possible for you and your MFR practice, book a "What's Possible" session with me and we can dream big and make your plan.

If you found this book to be helpful please share it with a friend. My goal is to help as many MFR therapists as possible, so they can help as many patients as possible.

NOTES

NOTES

NOTES

NOTES

NOTES

NOTES

NOTES

NOTES

NOTES

NOTES

NOTES

NOTES

NOTES

NOTES

NOTES

NOTES

Resources

Seminars

JOHN BARNES MYOFASCIAL RELEASE SEMINARS |
HTTPS://WWW.MYOFASCIALRELEASE.COM/SEMINARS
/ EMAIL: MALVERN@MYOFASCIALRELEASE.COM

MFR Therapists Directory

MARK BARNES| HTTP://MFRTHERAPISTS.COM/| EMAIL
CONTACT@MFRTHERAPISTS.COM

Profit U

ALEX ENGAR| AFFILIATE LINK:
HTTPS://WWW.PROFITUCOURSE.COM/PROFIT-
U/842W1 |

Made in the USA
Middletown, DE
05 November 2023

41907502R00066